Spirit Says...

BE INSPIRED

To Betty,
always be
inspired!
With Smiles,
Susan Bovas
:)

Spirit Says...

BE INSPIRED

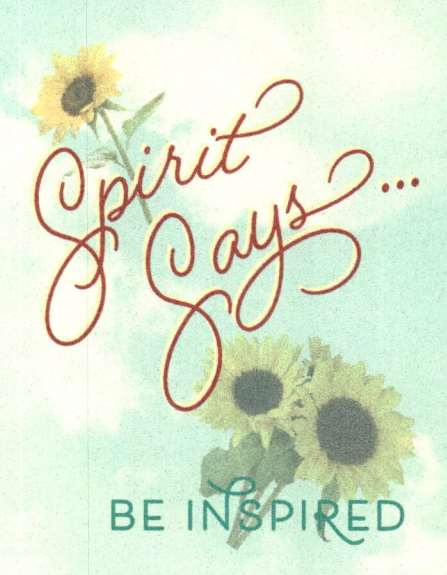

A COLLECTION *of*
ORIGINAL QUOTES
to
GUIDE YOUR LIFE'S PATH
with GENTLE WISDOM

DR. SUSAN BOVA

MARTIN AVENUE PRESS

Copyright © 2016 Susan Bova

All rights reserved. No part of this publication may be reproduced, distributed, or transmitted in any form or by any means, including photocopying, recording, digital scanning, or other electronic or mechanical methods, without the prior written permission of the publisher, except in the case of brief quotations embodied in critical reviews and certain other noncommercial uses permitted by copyright law.

Published 2016

ISBN: 978-1-945262-00-5
Library of Congress Control Number: 2016905897

Book design by Stacey Aaronson

Published by:
Martin Avenue Press
For inquiries, please address:
publisher@martinavenuepress.com

Printed in the United States of America

I remember ...
and so it begins.

A Note from the Author

Messages from guidance come in a variety of ways. Sometimes obvious. Sometimes cryptic. The cryptic messages are your guides nudging you to embrace your intuition, follow the clues, and let the story unfold in its own perfect way.

My guidance nudged me to share this wisdom with you. Each uplifting message is its own story waiting to unfold exactly the way you need it to in the moment.

It is my wish that these words inspire you to look beyond the ordinary and explore the world of endless possibilities.

Spirit says . . .

* there is no coincidence

* synchronicities are breadcrumbs left by the Universe showing you that all is as it should be

* don't second-guess the obvious . . . sometimes we make it easy!

Enjoy this gift of energy from a place of pure knowing ... and may you always be inspired!

With Smiles,
Susan

Spirit Says...

BE INSPIRED

Anything
is possible.
Don't wait until
the achievable
becomes so difficult
that you begin to
believe otherwise.

Confusion is often the *universe* telling you to take another look. There may be a *different* perspective that will bring *clarity* once you pay attention to what is less obvious.

Consider every perceived challenge as an *opportunity*. This will allow you to *stretch* the limits of your creativity and go above and *beyond* what you ever thought possible.

*D*on't waste the *present* moment by waiting for a future one. *Right now* is when life happens. So, when you *live* to see a *new day*, be sure to use that new day to live!

Don't be afraid
of making
the wrong choice.
Even wrong choices
are RIGHT when
you learn your life's
most important lessons.
Let your INTUITION
guide you.
Accept your choices
and go FORWARD
full speed ahead.

Excuses, Excuses ...
When you use
an excuse as a reason
to avoid doing something,
ask yourself if you
really want to do it at all.
When something is *right*,
and you really want it,
nothing should
get in your way.
So ... what is the excuse
really about?
And more importantly,
what do you *really*
want to do?

WHAT do you want to be when you grow up? We search and search for something that might interest us, when all we have to do is connect to our joy. We don't recognize what we're good at because it's so a part of who we are that it's not obvious to us. Pay attention to what you already love and your answer will be right in front of you.

✺

DO.

Stop waiting for
the perfect scenario.
When you wait,
you miss the
opportunities
that are immediately
available.

DO.

It is the order
of the time.

✺

*H*old a door *open*
for someone.
And, every once
in a while,
allow someone to
hold a door open for you.
It is just as important
to know how to *receive*
as it is to give.
So look for doors
to be opened,
welcome what is waiting
to be discovered,
and always remember
to say *thank you*.

The rational, logical mind is fear-based and less likely to take risks. It prevents us from following our inner guidance— the voice that leads us to bigger and greater things. Taking a leap without logic is necessary to experience the vastness of creation.

When you believe
you could *fly*,
if even for a moment,
find every way to
support your belief,
and *magically*,
you will
lift off.

SCARED DOES NOT MEAN STOP. WHEN THE *right circumstance* PRESENTS ITSELF, PUSH THROUGH THE FEAR OF UNCERTAINTY AND *be amazed* AT WHAT YOU ACCOMPLISH.

The time has come

to stop looking

for answers

outside yourself

and start becoming

what you are

looking for.

You don't need a reason to follow your INTUITION. Your intuition knows more than your intellectual mind. When you FEEL CALLED to do something and don't know why, DO IT anyway. The reason may present itself later. And even if it doesn't, following your intuition keeps you true to your AUTHENTIC SELF. Be the highest expression of who you TRULY are.

At times, we all get a sense of contentment, fulfillment, and *joy* within us, however brief or long. This is when your highest expression of self is speaking to you. During these times, your ***deepest desires*** are subtly manifesting. Questions are being answered in a quiet way. ***Pay attention*** to what is happening. ***Recognize*** the manifestations. And ***know*** that subtle answers are ***awesome*** answers because they settle in your essence naturally and ***joyfully***.

Look for the
true guidance
in your life,
however subtle,
and *know* that
the Universe
supports you.
You are
never alone.

A THOUGHT TO PONDER:
When you pray
for patience, and that's
exactly what you get,
why continue to
wonder why nothing
gets accomplished?
Jump into life with
full participation.
Because life will
surely pass you by
if all you do is observe
from the sidelines,
patiently.

Do not change to
please other people.
Change for your own
personal *growth*
and the
advancement of
your *soul*.

S hhh ...

Not having anything

to say

may be an indication

to simply not speak.

Having something to say

may indicate the same!

"Oh, that's nothing ..."
For those people who
always have it
worse than you,
and they make sure
you know it,
there is no need
to "one-up" them.
Let them have
that honor.
Then, add that you
are blessed to have
it good, and notice
the shift that occurs.

In THE GREAT MOVIE

OF *life*,

THE CASTING DIRECTOR

MADE THE *perfect* CHOICE.

YOU ARE THE ONLY ONE

QUALIFIED TO PLAY

THE ROLE OF *you*.

SO BE YOU — YOUR WAY.

AND TAKE FULL CREDIT

FOR THE *unique* PERSON

THAT YOU ARE.

YOU ARE A *star*!

When mediocre minds
take pleasure in making
you believe that "less"
is all there is,
it's time to align
with *stronger* minds
who will *support* and
encourage your
endeavors.

A smile is

a little bit of

sunshine.

Be sure to always

have one with you.

That way, even the

darkest days

will be a little

brighter.

Don't let the praise
or criticism from others
be your only
motivation to do or
not do something.
Let the ENCOURAGEMENT
from your HEART
for what feels right
be the guidance
in your life.
TRUST that
your heart knows
and ACT on that.

Enjoy the absence of
drama every now and then.
You don't always have to
have something going on.
Sometimes it's okay
to just say
"I'm letting life
show me what's next."
Then, take that break
from the drama and let
someone else be
queen for the day.

There may be a lot to learn from others, so put aside criticisms just long enough to to glean the gems you disguise as annoyances. Besides, those very others may be feeling the same about you ... and you're a fountain of enlightenment, aren't you?

Intuition
is not deep or cryptic.
It is an easy perk
in life.
Everyone has it,
some actively use it,
others expend a lot
of energy pretending
it's not there.
Surrender to your
intuitive self and let
the easy energy
lead the way.

Even when
everything may
seem gloomy,
there is always a
ray of light
shining somewhere —
you just have to
notice it.
So, focus on
something *positive*
today and watch
your world fill
with *brightness*.

Make a date with yourself
and get reacquainted.
Your intuition doesn't
always speak in a loud,
bold voice.
Sometimes the little,
subtle whispers are
the ones that lead you to
great accomplishments.
When you know the voice
of your highest self,
and you follow it,
great things happen.
So make that date and
be the best listener.
You'll be amazed
with the wisdom
you will hear!

Your body REGISTERS
THE ENERGETIC FIELD
AROUND YOU.
YOU CAN FEEL
AND SENSE
WHAT WILL HAPPEN
BEFORE AN ACTUAL
EVENT OCCURS.
AND THAT "HUNCH" –
IT'S YOUR INNER VOICE
TELLING YOU TO
PAY ATTENTION
TO THE CUES.
Tune in.
YOU KNOW MORE
THAN YOU REALIZE.

Keep buying green bananas. That way, you always have something to look forward to.

Your SIXTH SENSE comes from what seems like nowhere and is often overlooked because there is no logic associated with it. Answers are readily available when you stop searching and waiting. Get quiet, stop thinking, and DISCOVER how the void is so much more than an empty space. It is filled with all the answers you need, ANSWERS that are impossible to gather while in your thinking mind.

The person you see in the mirror every day is the person you live with the most.

Be Kind.

Find a way to like that person. A good friend is waiting to be discovered ... and the potential for a lasting relationship is likely.

Hello beautiful!

You are not
what other
people call you.
You are what
you answer to.
Do not accept the
limits imposed on you
by yourself and others.
Break through
limitations
and be *free*.

When you are at a
loss for words,
stop thinking and
let the silence speak.
When the mental chatter
calms down,
the answers will be
right there
waiting for you
to notice them.

Sometimes, to get unstuck, you need to give yourself permission to be *authentic*. Knowing and understanding your unique qualities will open *new horizons* for you. Be **you** rather than what you think the world wants you to be.

When you fall down,
you have the opportunity
to get back up and
start again ...
Maybe differently,
maybe better,
maybe from a
new perspective ...
And maybe falling down
is exactly what you need –
to shake up the energy –
to get you out
of complacency.
So get up, get on with it,
and remember
to smile!

Everyone has *unique* gifts and talents. Know what yours are and appreciate that you have them. *Be confident!* Hold true to your uniqueness and the Universe will open with *unlimited* opportunities.

It is easy
to find your way
to the top
once you learn
to find your way
through the crowd
at the bottom.
Break away from
what holds you back
and watch
your world
expand.

For a moment,
let yourself imagine
beyond what you
were conditioned
to believe.
When you *imagine*
there has to be
more, there is!
Don't accept
the belief that
any limit is all
there is ...
and that includes
the sky!

Sometimes there are things you just know innately, without question.
Is what you *know* in line with what you *do*?
Are your actions in sync with what your highest guidance is telling you?
Take a few moments to *check in* ...
your wisdom is waiting to be heard!

Life should be
like a comfortable
pair of boots:
a place for great
"soul" support,
warm enough to
keep you smiling,
able to take you
on many journeys,
when broken in,
it becomes better,
and, when necessary,
with an opening
long enough to
zip it shut!

Be aware OF THE SUBTLE ENERGY SURROUNDING YOU. THIS IS YOUR ETHERIC BODY – THE ENERGY THAT INFORMS YOU OF WHAT IS TO BE – EVEN BEFORE THE OCCURRENCE EXISTS ON THE PHYSICAL PLANE.

Every dream is a possibility.
When you dream something,
it has already taken flight
and mingled with
Universal creation.
Dream **BIG** and let
the Universe begin its
manifestation for you.
When you dream
a dream, claim it;
make it your own.
Don't shoot it to the moon
for someone else
to capture.
You are worthy of
dreaming **BIG** and making
your dreams ... **YOURS!**

When you shine
your light bright
for all to see,
you will attract
all kinds of
critters,
even those wanting
to make mischief.
That doesn't mean
to dim your light
to keep them away.
Au contraire!
Shine it even
brighter and just
keep glowing!

It is okay to ask for help
even when your life's mission
is to go it alone.
Getting over a major hurdle
may be as easy as
accepting help rather than
struggling alone.
Even the slightest relief
from your burden will
bring you enormous
peace of mind.
Accepting help allows
a fresh perspective,
which can bring solutions
you may otherwise never know.
Be open and receive.

Don't wait for the perfect scenario to allow yourself to be happy. Happiness is not conditional. *Choose to be happy* without a reason and every scenario will be perfect!

SOMETIMES HOPE
CAN BE FORTIFIED

WITH ACTION.

TAKE PART IN

YOUR DESTINY BY

TAKING ACTION –

NOW.

Look at people for who
they are, not for who
you want them to be.
When you see people for
who you want them to be,
you miss the opportunity
to know the *uniqueness*
of each person.
We are all uniquely different ...
perfect in our own
special ways.
Find a bit of perfection
in everyone and
celebrate the specialty
each person brings
to this lifetime.

DO WHATEVER
IS NECESSARY,
IN A SAFE AND
HEALTHY WAY,
TO *achieve* WHAT
YOU TRULY DESIRE.
YOU HAVE THE
ABILITY TO DO WHAT
YOU NEED TO DO.
JUST ASK YOURSELF
WHAT IT IS THAT
YOU TRULY DESIRE,
WHAT BEST SERVES
YOUR *highest purpose*.
WHEN YOU KNOW
WHAT THAT IS,
RESOURCES APPEAR
TO HELP MAKE IT SO.

Life is like swimming.
When you jump in
with an inner tube,
flapping and kicking,
you won't go very far.
Dive in the deep end
and feel the whoosh
of exhilaration ...
When you come up
for a breath, much
will be accomplished.
Go for it !!!

RATIONALIZATION
AND LOGICAL THINKING
ARE SURE WAYS TO
STOP THE FORWARD
MOMENTUM OF AN
EXTRAORDINARY LIFE.
THE GREATEST
ACCOMPLISHMENTS
ARE BORN WHEN YOU
take intuitive action.
YOU DON'T ALWAYS
HAVE TO KNOW HOW
TO DO SOMETHING.
JUST MOVE TOWARD IT.
TAKE THE FIRST STEP
AND THE NEXT STEP
WILL BE REVEALED.
TRUST THAT ALL
IS WELL.

It is not necessary

to be fearless.

We all have fear.

It is more important

to recognize that

fear exists and then

move forward

anyway.

What do you believe without question? It is important to know what drives you because those may be the very fundamentals that hold you back. Know what beliefs shape your existence, then question if those beliefs support your *authentic self* or pull you away from who you really are.

Sometimes the
Universe
steps in and directs
the course of life
despite our human
attempts to orchestrate it
to what we believe
it should be.
These are the times
to relinquish control
and go along for the ride.
Grander things await.
Trust in the
Greater Power
and know that
all is well!

To access the
limitless possibilities
available to you,
you have to engage
your sixth sense.
It is a crucial component
in discovering the
greatness that awaits you.
Start by adopting
the belief that
ANYTHING IS POSSIBLE.
Then, accept and welcome
all the joys and
happy surprises the
universe sends your way.
Belief in your heart
is the way to start.
And a smile is
always worthwhile.
May you have a happy start
to a wondrous day!

Failure is not the person. Failure is merely a misconception, a situation that is different from what we wanted or expected. In every perceived failure, there is *wisdom*. And wise is the soul.

In due time,
when the time is right,
all will be made
known to you.
When you struggle
to understand
what is to be –
it is not to be.
When the time is right,
you will *know*
in every fiber
of your being.
That is the time to
embrace the knowing.
Let the doing begin.

If your eyes are
windows to your soul,
then your mouth
is the door.
So feed your soul
kindness
by opening with
a smile
rather than looking
with a scowl and
clouding the view.

ABUNDANCE,
WEALTH, AND
FORTUNE
ARE THE BIRTHRIGHTS
OF EACH ONE OF US.
WHAT TROUBLES DO
YOU CREATE TO
PREVENT THEM FROM
MANIFESTING IN
IN YOUR LIFE?
Accept ABUNDANCE,
invite WEALTH,
claim YOUR FORTUNE.
THERE IS PLENTY
FOR EVERYONE.
Be worthy
AND LET THEM BE YOURS!

Be open to the possibility that sometimes souls come back for a visit ... to calm a fear, to bring a message, or just to say hello. Not believing doesn't mean it doesn't happen. It just puts the probability out of your range of vision.
Be receptive!
Witness the world beyond your five senses. There's a lot going on that you can tap into once you let yourself *believe!*

The present moment
IS WHAT WE HAVE.
WHY WAIT FOR A
MILESTONE NUMBER
TO REMINISCE?
A HAPPY EVENT
ISN'T ANY HAPPIER
IN FIVE- OR TEN-YEAR
INCREMENTS.
DON'T CONTAIN
YOUR HAPPINESS FOR
A MILESTONE NUMBER.
CELEBRATE EVERY DAY,
now!

Weird is simply being wired differently.
Same letters,
different configuration.
It's a good thing!
It's creative.
It's unique.
Express the weirdness
in you ...
Be creative
and disconnect from
your wired network.
Ahhh ...

TAKE TIME
TO LOOK IN
THE MIRROR TODAY
AND
THANK YOURSELF
FOR BEING
THE *awesome*
PERSON THAT
YOU ARE.

It is okay to
ask for something
you want.
Be sure you
really want what
you ask for.
Also, be open to
other possibilities
that may be
even better.
P.S. Consider asking
for something
that isn't material.

Choose You!

In the playground of life,
stop waiting for
your name to be called.
Go out and play
your own game,
your own way,
in the manner you
were meant to play.
Be the first to
choose yourself.
That way, your team
will always have the
BEST!

When your path
is paved with ease,
accept that as fact,
and know that's how it's
supposed to be at that time.
Do not allow room for guilt
just because those around you
may be experiencing hardship,
struggle, or be engrossed
in "poor me's."
Recognize and embrace
the goodness the universe
sets forth for you and
be an example for others
to also recognize and accept
the positive experiences
in their lives.
Know that All Is Well.

Sometimes a closed door is an invitation to reopen it.
The old way was under construction and you have been kept out to avoid breathing the dust.
If it feels right, reopen the door and *explore the possibilities* waiting for you.

REMEMBER: WE ARE ALL SOULS TEMPORARILY HOUSED IN HUMAN BODIES. WHEN IT'S TIME TO MOVE ON, WHAT STORY WILL YOUR SOUL BRING WITH IT? THERE ARE STILL CHAPTERS LEFT TO BE WRITTEN. MAKE THEM *spectacular*!

Stop stressing!
What you are doing *right now* is what
is being done.
Everything else is
not happening.
So, right now,
pick one thing that
will make a difference
in a *positive* way;
one thing in the present
that makes you feel good.
Because when you
feel good,
that positive energy
spreads to others.
And so it begins …

Consciously be *nice*.

Do it

over and over again

until it becomes

so ingrained in you

that it becomes

an unconscious

and *everyday* act.

Do you ever feel there is *more* to life than what you experience? When you are not satisfied with how your life is going —

GOOD!

Sometimes this awareness is what you need to *motivate* you to do something different. This change may be what will *catapult* you to the great place you are meant to be.

If we must reflect
on the past, be sure
to include the fundamentals
of kindergarten:
play nice,
use your inside voice,
and take a nap.
Translated to the present:
smile, listen to your
intuition (the voice within),
and take a nap.
Ahhh ... good idea!

When you're
feeling unsettled
and scattered,
you are in a cycle
of *change*.
This is a time to
examine new choices
that present themselves
to you as you shift
into a *new experience*.
You have the
opportunity to choose
the option that
best matches
the new you that
is waiting to *blossom*.
It's a good time
for change.

DON'T WAIT FOR
A SPECIAL DAY
TO DO SOMETHING
NICE FOR SOMEONE.
MAKE SOMEONE
FEEL SPECIAL
"JUST BECAUSE"
AND DO IT
IN THE MOMENT.
IT IS GOOD
FOR THE SOUL!

The world goes on.

It's a new day.

What positive change

occurred for you that

is different from yesterday?

Create a difference:

Smile more consciously.

Take a moment to be

grateful for at least

one small goodness

in your life.

And know that

All Is Well.

When you have a
CREATIVE IDEA,
don't stop pursuing it
because you have no
support or facts backing it.
Every new idea begins
without support or it
wouldn't be new.
It all starts with your
creative self.
So use your
IMAGINATION,
create the next masterpiece.
Then, let your enthusiasm
and excitement become
the support you need.

The most valuable
piece of real estate
is the one we live in
every day —
the *human body*.
Keep it updated,
rejuvenated,
clean and spiffy.
You never know when
it'll be called
for an appraisal.

BELIEF + REPETITION = TRUTH.
WHEN YOU CHOOSE TO
BELIEVE SOMETHING
AND YOU ACT ON IT
OVER AND OVER,
IT BECOMES
REALITY FOR YOU.
SO, TODAY, CHOOSE TO
believe something good,
SOMETHING POSITIVE.
THEN, REPEAT IT
OVER AND OVER
UNTIL THAT, TOO,
BECOMES TRUE
FOR YOU.

Dreams
are not just
for sleep time.
Our best dreams
are those we have
while we are awake.
So, dream big,
dream often,
and make your
dreams exactly
the way you
want them to be.

What positive
thoughts and ideas
are you keeping
to yourself?
It does your spirit good to
share positive energy
so all can benefit.
The Universe rewards you
by returning the energy
a thousand-fold
and in multiple ways!

A small change

is all that's necessary

to make a remarkable

difference in

one's perspective.

For example:

change two letters

in "idiot" and you get

idoit – I do it.

Small change,

BIG difference.

Your abilities
are yours.
No other person
can use them.
How powerful it is
to know that you
can do at least one thing
no one else can do –
exactly the way you do it.
Be confident!
You are somebody
uniquely important.
Do your thing!

It is better
to do something
and be wrong
than to never do
anything at all.
That way you at least
gain experience
from which to grow.

Be fearless.

Bring your passion
to life.

Signs or Tests ...
Do obstacles keep
popping up when you're
wanting to do something?
Maybe they're signs
guiding you away
from doing that.
OR ...
Maybe they're tests
of your perseverance
to go after your dream
no matter what.
There is a difference.
Can you be quiet enough
to know which one
it is for you?

As you get closer to realizing your heart's desire, obstacles show up to test your resolve. Keep going. You are worthy of achieving your dream.

When you wait
for others to make
you great,
you will often be
let down and
disappointed.
Go for your
own greatness.
Create it yourself.
Stop waiting.
Stop hoping.
YOU start
the momentum.
Be involved ...
That's the only way
to ensure the results
you want.

When you stop
at your limit, the world
still moves on –
just not
with you anymore ...
because you believed
what you perceived to be
all there is.
In fact, there is more.
Go *beyond* your limits.
Find your more
and then *go for it*!

A gentle reminder:
Every now and then
take a few moments
to sit quietly.
Detach from your thoughts
and let them pass by
without reacting.
Breathe deeply and slowly
and just BE.
Your day will still be there
with all its demands,
only now you'll have
more energy to embrace it.
BREATHE and recharge –
it really works
to your advantage!

Intuition is
mistakenly believed
to only be inside
one's being, when it
actually includes
an outward extension
of all things possible.
Go beyond
inner belief and bring
your wisdom out
into the world.
People are waiting to
embrace your genius.

When you create
a space of loneliness
for yourself,
it is difficult to know
the truth of how
your situation actually is.
🍃 That's because
all you look for is
proof of isolation
while the bliss is
all around you. 🍃
Bring the bliss within
and find the joy
of being you.

Every once in a while
take time from your
busy, hectic schedule
to simply do nothing.
Stop for a while
and just BE.
Your worries and
responsibilities will
still be there –
only now you'll have a
refreshed spirit
that supports you on
your life's journey
rather than a
suppressed spirit that is
unknowlingly tucked away.
Do nothing and just BE ...
Ahhh ...

Remember ...
WHEN IT RAINS,
THE SUN STILL SHINES
ABOVE THE CLOUDS.
SO WHEN YOU
FEEL GLOOMY,
PULL YOURSELF UP.
Rise above
YOUR CLOUDY FORECAST.
Glow IN THE LIGHT
OF YOUR OWN SUNSHINE.
IT'S ALWAYS THERE.
JUST REMEMBER TO
reach above
THE CLOUDS ...
AND SMILE!!!

No need to
connect the dots.
Just step back and look
with amazement
at the entire picture
you already created.
Each dot is a part of the
wonder of life
and it leads you
forward.
The connection
is already there.

There is
always something
about us that is
perfect.
we just spend
so much time
picking on the
imperfections
that we come
to believe
there is
nothing else.

There is no
next step until
the first step
is taken.
Waiting
and wondering
will not make
it happen.
So just
take the first step
and the next step
will follow.
Ready, set, GO!

When you want to do something right, stop worrying about doing it wrong.

*In the midst of chaos,
hustle and bustle,
juggling schedules,
when there's more to do
than there's time
to do it,
these are the times
to stop for a moment,
take a breath,
clear your mind,
and know that
All Is Well...
All Is Well.*

You don't have to
experience a happy
event in order to SMILE.
You can choose to ✿
smile anytime, anywhere,
with minimal effort.
Consider smiling as a dose
of feel-good medicine —
✿ no cost and
no prescription needed.
Possible side effects:
make a friend, calm a fear,
lift a spirit, ✿
expand a horizon,
encourage an ahhh ...
Note: highly contagious;
✿ may cause a
positive environment;
may create a happy event.

Moments of clarity
happen in
an instant and
are often disregarded
as nonsense.
It is those moments
of clarity,
when acted upon,
that usher in
greatness.

Be clear.
Be in the moment.

*A*RE YOU STUCK WITH WHAT YOUR BRAIN WANTS YOU TO BELIEVE? ARE YOU TRAPPED INSIDE THE BOX CREATED BY YOUR EGO? WHEN YOU ARE LIMITED TO THE CREATIONS OF HUMAN CAPACITY, LIFE CAN SEEM IMPOSSIBLE. YOU LIMIT YOUR ABILITIES TO LOOK BEYOND WHAT IS PRESENTED TO YOU. *Stretch your limits* AND GO BEYOND THE FIVE SENSES. TURN "IMPOSSIBLE" TO: "*I*" "m" "*Possible.*"

Tomorrow,
next week,
later, sometime,
someday = never.
When you have
an idea,
act on it NOW.
When you want
to do something,
start doing it NOW.
Ideas become
invaluable when
they are acted upon.
Take action —
NOW.

Even when

CLOUDS OF DOUBT

CAST SHADOWS ON

THE SPROUTS OF

NEWLY PLANTED SEEDS,

DO NOT FALTER.

THEN COMES THE RAIN

THAT WATERS THE SEEDS

AND THE SEEDS *blossom*

INTO MIGHTY TREES ...

WHICH, THEN, BASK

IN SUNLIGHT

AND WITHSTAND

THE STORMS.

Grow your dreams!

The best way to get something done is to start doing it. Aww, what's one more day? 🍂 One day becomes a week and then a month ... and you're still waiting to start. 🍂 Geesh! You could have been a month ahead if you would have just started back then! *Now* is the future date you were waiting for a month ago. 🍂 So, start already!

When you
DESIRE CHANGE
and nothing seems
to happen, take heart.
Just as seeds lie dormant
under the ground,
much activity takes place
on a non-sensory level.
Invisible to the eye,
seedlings grow.
Suddenly, flowers bloom
and NEW LIFE arises.
So, too, for us.
When we plant the seeds
of change and let the
UNIVERSE work its MAGIC,
new life will arise.
Trust that all is well.
Arise and greet your
NEW BEGINNING.

Look at people for who they are, not for what you want them to be. Then, rather than be disappointed, *be excited* for the unique points of view others bring to your world.

Be the author of your own story. It's better than reading about it in someone else's book.

SOMETIMES
YOU NEED TO
STOP TALKING
AND LET THE
natural flow
OF LIFE
LEAD THE WAY.
YOU WILL DISCOVER
A LOT WHEN
YOU GET
OUT OF YOUR
OWN WAY.

Your intuition IS YOUR BEST TEACHER. DON'T SETTLE FOR SOMETHING JUST BECAUSE SOMEONE ELSE SAID YOU SHOULD. KNOW THE *wise voice* OF YOUR INTUITION VS. THE DESIRE OF ANOTHER TELLING YOU WHAT IS BEST. BE INFORMED. *Be empowered.* LISTEN TO YOUR INNER VOICE.

Look at limits
for what they
actually may be:
excuses to prevent you
from reaching
greatness.
Limits are safety nets
to prevent you from
doing *better* than you
are comfortable doing.
Leave your comfort zone,
break free
from your limits,
and find your
greatness.

Do not be
deceived by something
your mind
convinced you to do.
It is better to know
with your heart
than to be convinced
with your mind.

♡

When you are called to do your *soul's work*, you often have to give up some actions, lifestyles, and even people that hold you back. This can be frightening, lonely, and dismissive for many. Just know that, in the long run, the *bliss* of choosing your path will far outweigh the angst of separation.

*D*o not just
follow your dream ...
that keeps you
always behind it,
looking at it
from a distance,
and at an arm's
length away from
experiencing it.
Only "following"
your dream gives
you so many
"acceptable" excuses
for not living it.
Dream it,
catch it, live it —
and don't make
new excuses for
succeeding at it!

When spark and motivation seem to fade, it is *imperative* to keep on going. Your energy is shifting into higher gear and you are feeling the void in the action. Take that time to *nurture* and *fortify* yourself so you can be ready for round two or three or ten or twenty. Consider it down time rather than a time to be down. *Keep going*.

Your environment
is an extension
of your mind.
Your thoughts
create your reality.
BE GREATER
than your environment
by changing how
you think about it.

Answers OFTEN
COME IN SUBTLE WAYS.
AND SOMETIMES
ANSWERS ARE SO
OBVIOUS THAT
THEY ARE OVERLOOKED.
Pay attention
TO ALL ENERGIES
THAT MANIFEST IN
YOUR SENSORY WORLD.
OTHERWISE, YOU
MAY BE MISSING OUT
ON AN EASY,
SMOOTH TRANSITION
INTO AN
extraordinary life!

When you feel stuck, do one thing differently. When you find your world doesn't crumble (or even if it does), you have the *power* to make a second, new choice. There is life *beyond* what is familiar.

Do you recognize
when the Universe
nudges you along?
It could be
misconstrued as
upheaval, chaos,
change.
Rather than fight it,
live your way through it
and discover
the wonders that
are there for you
to *embrace*.

When I think,
I do not create.

The thinking mind
judges, criticizes,
and makes excuses.

The creative mind
does it anyway,
no matter what.

Create your masterpiece –
no ifs, buts,
or thoughts about it.

When you have

a challenging day

and nothing seems

to go right,

go out and do

something good for

somebody else.

Serving others is

a great way to

lift your spirit and

elevate your mood.

Just once, take a *leap of faith* and let answers come to you rather than figuring out a solution that fits into your limited parameters. This allows the knowing to occur without explanation. Even in chaos, *All Is Well.*

Are you doing
the same things
the same way you
did them a year ago?
Five years ago?
Ten years ago?
And wonder why
you're not
getting anywhere?
First, ask where it is
you want to
be "getting."
Then, if what you're
doing is contrary to
where you want to go,
hmm ...
might be time
to make a change.

"POTENTIAL" IS

ALWAYS LURKING

IN THE FUTURE

AND IS CONSEQUENTLY

ALWAYS OUT OF REACH.

WHEN YOU ARE

AWARE OF

YOUR POTENTIAL,

ACT ON IT NOW

AND MAKE IT

A REALITY.

We all have an etheric GPS – our internal guidance system. The instruction:
START MOVING!
You will not be told where to turn in two miles until you start the two-mile drive. To know where to turn, what path to take, you must start moving first. The next step will only be given after you start the journey.
Bottom line: Take the first step and the next step appears.

Learn how to *pay attention* now.
That way you
won't miss the
moments between
dreaming of what
you want and
achieving it.
Be aware and alive
even during the times
nothing seems
to happen.

While we cannot control the temperature outside, we can always control the temperament inside.

Endings are
simply the
Universe telling you
it's time to start
something **new**.
You've completed a cycle.
The energy frequency
is elevated to a
more ***expansive*** space.
There is now
more room
for you to ***soar***.

Acknowledgments

Thank you to everyone who supported my life's path leading up to this creation.

Hugs and kisses to all my family here on earth, with a special smile to Mom, Carol, Barbara, Rachel, Nicole, Shelly, Debbie, Jude, and Lil' Red.

To all my family now watching from the Spirit plane, especially Dad, Pop, and my mentor Romy. I know you witness this from a grander perspective. Keep the energy flowing.

George, my go-to idea guy, yay baybay!

To Jeffrey Stiglich, Katie Blanc, Marianne Bodnar, Debbie Hofkamp, and Jacqueline Devaney, I truly appreciate your valuable insight.

Blessings to my supporters who read and like my quotes on FB – this is where it started. You inspire me to keep on going.

To Stacey Aaronson, my visionary guide. You created a masterpiece beyond what I ever imagined. I am blessed to know you.

Thank you Spirit! Without your guidance, these words would never have appeared.

And to my husband, Jim, who journeys with me, you are truly an angel in human form! LUA

About the Author

author photo by Rachel

Susan Bova, PhD, is a doctor of holistic health, a visionary, a seer, and an intuitive healer. Her mission is to motivate, educate, and inspire others to achieve optimal states in mind, body, and spirit, and to fully engage their sixth-sensory intuitive sides. As an inspirational speaker, Susan combines wisdom with humor to gently encourage others to expand their horizons, welcome new perspectives, and embrace intuition. She runs a private practice in suburban Chicago.

www.drsusanbova.com

For more inspiring quotes, visit Susan's Facebook page at:
facebook.com/DrSusanBova